KEVIN JOHNSON

SOAR

FLY INTO GOD'S PLAN FOR YOUR FUTURE

HIGHER
SERIES

ZONDERVAN®

ZONDERVAN.com/
AUTHORTRACKER
follow your favorite authors

youth
specialties

YOUTH SPECIALTIES

Soar: Fly into God's Plan for Your Future
Copyright 2009 by Kevin Johnson

Youth Specialties resources, 300 S. Pierce St., El Cajon, CA 92020 are published by Zondervan, 5300 Patterson Ave. SE, Grand Rapids, MI 49530.

ISBN 978-0-310-28267-9

Cover design by David Conn
Interior design by SharpSeven Design

Printed in the United States of America

09 10 11 12 13 14 • 20 19 18 17 16 15 14 13 12 11 10 9 8 7 6 5 4 3 2 1

Contents

Start Here

It's time to let your faith fly HIGHER. If you're ready to take your relationship with God to the next level, this series of books shows you how.

Soar contains 20 Bible studies that lead you upward. You'll find Scriptures that speak to the core of your life, along with space to express what's on your mind. You'll think for yourself and uncover significant insights you might not find on your own. *Soar* shows you how to discover God's plan for your life—from major decisions to minor details. You'll find out how glad God is to guide you. And you'll figure out for yourself why you don't want to settle for anything less.

Don't rush through *Soar*. You can do a study per day, a study per week, or anything between. Actually, the slower you go, the more you'll gain. Each study is just a few pages long but provides you plenty to think about and act upon. The end of each study comes with added material to let you fly even higher.

You'll see that every study opens with a mostly-blank page that has a single Bible verse that sums up the main point. These verses are worth memorizing, as a way to fill your head with the amazing truths of God's Word. Then comes **START**, a brief introduction to get you into the topic. **READ** takes you to a Scripture passage. You can read the verses here in the book or, if you want, grab your own Bible and read the passage there. **THINK** helps you examine the main ideas of the text, and **LIVE** makes it easy to apply what you learn. **WRAP** pulls everything together.

Then there's some bonus material. **MORE THOUGHTS TO MULL** tosses you a few more questions to ask yourself or others. **MORE SCRIPTURES TO DIG** leads you to related Bible passages to help you hear even more from God on the topic.

Whether you read on your own or get together with a group, *Soar* will help your faith fly high. It's your chance to grab the best that God has in store for you.

Kevin Johnson

1. WHO KNOWS YOU?

God sees the true you

Psalm 139:1

You have searched me, Lord, and
you know me.

START Maybe your teachers actually can tell when your brain wanders. Maybe your coach really does know when you bend the team code of conduct. And maybe your brother truly is streaming your life to the world by webcam. While you probably don't want everything you've ever thought or done shown in public, there's still good reason to be glad when the right person can see right through you. Like the doctor who shines a bright light in dark places, the friend who spots your hurts a mile away, or the parent who anticipates your every need. Sometimes you want your privacy invaded. It all depends on who's doing the invading.

Whom do you trust enough to let into your life? How much do you let them see of the real you?

READ Psalm 139:1-6, 13-16

> [1] You have searched me, Lord, and you know me. [2] You know when I sit and when I rise; you perceive my thoughts from afar. [3] You discern my going out and my lying down; you are familiar with all my ways. [4] Before a word is on my tongue you, Lord, know it completely. [5] You hem me in behind and before, and you lay your hand upon me. [6] Such knowledge is too wonderful for me, too lofty for me to attain. [13] For you created my inmost being; you knit me together in my mother's womb. [14] I praise you because I am fearfully and wonderfully made; your works are wonderful, I know that full well. [15] My frame was not hidden from you when I was made in the secret place. When I was woven together in the depths of the earth, [16] your eyes saw my unformed body. All the days ordained for me were written in your book before one of them came to be.

THINK Psalm 139 was written by a guy who experienced both soaring highs and crashing lows in his relationship with God. As King of Israel around 1000 BC, David was a believer known for having God's heart (Acts 13:22); yet he was also a betrayer who sent a loyal soldier to his death so he could marry the man's wife (2 Samuel 11:15).

What exactly does God know about David—and about you? Jot a list from Psalm 139.

How does God know all these things?

God knows you inside and out. He saw you even before you were born, and he's watched you every day since. He has even seen your whole life ahead of time. By the way, that word *fearfully* in verse 14 means "awe-strikingly." God's handiwork is unquestionably great, and he knew exactly what he was doing when you were being assembled in your mother's womb.

You'd think David would run from the roving eye of God. But he doesn't sound scared. Why not?

LIVE Of all the people in the world, who knows you the best? Is that a good thing? Why—or why not?

Who knows things about you that you wish no one knew? How does *that* feel?

God knows you completely. What do you think about that fact?

WRAP It's amazing: Do something, God saw it. Say something, God heard it. Think something, God knows it. What's even more amazing is that this God wants a relationship with you and uses his all-knowing power for your good. He knows exactly what you need.

» MORE THOUGHTS TO MULL

- Do you think God actually knows you this well—or have you somehow escaped his notice? Why do you think that?

- Would you hide from God if you could? Why—or why not?

- Ask your mom or dad if they saw an ultrasound picture of you before you were born. If so, how did they feel when they saw that first fuzzy image of you? Or what did they feel when they knew you were on the way?

» MORE SCRIPTURES TO DIG

- David wasn't perfect. Even though he had reason to hide from God, at the end of Psalm 139 he invited God's scrutiny. He says, "Search me, God, and know my heart; test me and know my anxious thoughts. See if there is any offensive way in me, and lead me in the way everlasting" (**Psalm 139:23-24**). He saw God's knowledge of him as the first step to God remaking his life for the better.

- God knows everything about you—good, bad, or completely ugly. Yet even when God sees you at your worst, he still loves you. In fact, **Romans 5:8** says, "God demonstrates his own love for us in this: While we were still sinners, Christ died for us."

- The fact that God knows everything—his "omniscience"—might be a terrifying thought. David flipped that fear on its head. He wrote, "How precious to me are your thoughts, God!" (**Psalm 139:17**). He was glad to discover that God was always near, even in the dark of night (**Psalm 139:18**).

2. YOUR BRIGHT FUTURE

God has amazing plans for you

Jeremiah 29:11

"For I know the plans I have for you," declares the Lord, "plans to prosper you and not to harm you, plans to give you hope and a future."

START Some people imagine that God's biggest concern is inventing point-less rules and punishing people who mess up. These people believe that if there's the slightest chance God has caught you being naughty rather than nice, you may as well give up hoping that he has anything good in store for you.

Do you think that God wants to wreck your life? Why—or why not?

READ Jeremiah 29:11-14

> [11] "For I know the plans I have for you," declares the Lord, "plans to prosper you and not to harm you, plans to give you hope and a future. [12] Then you will call on me and come and pray to me, and I will listen to you. [13] You will seek me and find me when you seek me with all your heart. [14] I will be found by you," declares the Lord, "and will bring you back from captivity. I will gather you from all the nations and places where I have banished you," declares the Lord, "and will bring you back to the place from which I carried you into exile."

THINK God spoke these words to his brokenhearted people. As individuals and as a nation, they had rebelled against God, disobeying his commands. After centuries of refusing to follow God, they'd been conquered by an invad-ing army and carried off as war trophies to the ancient city of Babylon. When they were at their most down-and-out, God gave them this message through the prophet Jeremiah.

What kind of plans does God have for his people?

What all does God promise them?

God had allowed people to experience the consequences of their sin. But what does he have in store for them?

LIVE When have you felt confident God wants the best for you? When have you worried that God is out to get you?

You might dream up a stack of reasons God can't or won't be kind to you. But this promise of a good plan and a bright future isn't just for Old Testament folks. It's also for you.

How do you think God defines the "good plan" he has for you? Is his definition the same as yours?

Given the bad publicity God often gets, why would you believe he has good plans for you?

If God is on your side, why doesn't life always go the way you want?

WRAP Here's one of the most basic questions you could ever ask or answer: Is God for you—or against you? God himself promises you can trust him to do you good. Whether you've lived close to him or wandered far away, God wants to lead you onward and upward. He wants to teach you to soar.

» MORE THOUGHTS TO MULL

- Was God being good to his people when he let them face the consequences of their sin?

- Why are some people afraid of God? Should they be? Explain.

- How do you think you discover God's good plans?

» MORE SCRIPTURES TO DIG

- The Bible asserts that God's care extends to all people of earth. Jesus said that God "causes his sun to rise on the evil and the good, and sends rain on the righteous and the unrighteous" (**Matthew 5:45**). Rain might sound like a party-stopper, but everyone listening to Jesus understood rain was a gift that brought life to their parched desert environment. And Paul wrote that God showers his rich kindness, tolerance, and patience on all people to prompt them to turn from evil and obey him (**Romans 2:4**).

- In **John 10:10** Jesus explained why he came to earth, and his reason might surprise you. He said, "I have come that they may have life, and have it to the full."

- Don't miss **Romans 8:38-39**, which says God's best plans for you come together in Christ. Nothing in the world can separate you "from the love of God that is in Christ Jesus our Lord."

3. FIRST THINGS FIRST

Seek God

Matthew 6:33

But seek first his kingdom and his righteousness, and all these things will be given to you as well.

START Picture yourself paused at a fork in a road, a place where you must choose between going one way or the other. Heading down one path means doing life your own way—going where you wish and doing what you want. The other road means making a fresh start with God, following him in whatever he has planned for you. Now consider this: You stand at that decision point continually, whether you're making major life plans or just deciding what to do with your weekend. With every pick you make, you're either choosing to go God's way—or your own.

Before you lies a choice between a) the greatest plans you can imagine for yourself and b) the greatest plans God can dream up. Which do you pick—and why?

READ Matthew 6:28-34

28 "And why do you worry about clothes? See how the flowers of the field grow. They do not labor or spin. 29 Yet I tell you that not even Solomon in all his splendor was dressed like one of these. 30 If that is how God clothes the grass of the field, which is here today and tomorrow is thrown into the fire, will he not much more clothe you—you of little faith? 31 So do not worry, saying, 'What shall we eat?' or 'What shall we drink?' or 'What shall we wear?' 32 For the pagans run after all these things, and your heavenly Father knows that you need them. 33 But seek first his kingdom and his righteousness, and all these things will be given to you as well. 34 Therefore do not worry about tomorrow, for tomorrow will worry about itself. Each day has enough trouble of its own."

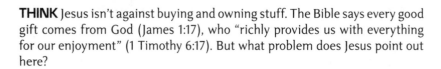

THINK Jesus isn't against buying and owning stuff. The Bible says every good gift comes from God (James 1:17), who "richly provides us with everything for our enjoyment" (1 Timothy 6:17). But what problem does Jesus point out here?

Earlier in this passage Jesus noted that sooner or later all earthly things get stolen or break (Matthew 6:19). Instead of making possessions your highest priority in life, you can store up "treasure in heaven" (Matthew 6:20).

Why shouldn't you worry?

What does Jesus want the main focus of your life to be? What will happen if you make that your goal?

"His kingdom" means letting God rule every moment of your life. In this passage "his righteousness" means doing life God's way, following his plans and commands. Material stuff, by the way, isn't the only distraction that can keep us from paying attention to God. But organizing life around the things and experiences money can buy—well, that's a major way God gets bumped out of life.

LIVE How much time, money, and energy do you spend getting more and better things?

How does your relationship with God suffer when possessions become your focus?

What does it mean for you to "seek first" God's kingdom? How are you doing that?

WRAP God invites you to live close to him, to enjoy his presence and power in every moment of your life. But that won't happen if your big plans and everyday choices don't include him.

» MORE THOUGHTS TO MULL

- How can you use the things you own and enjoy to help you get closer to God?

- When do you experience pressure to accumulate things?

- Take some time today to scan your stuff—and your schedule. Has any of it become more important to you than God? How do you know God's at the top of your list of what you want out of life?

» MORE SCRIPTURES TO DIG

- Read **Philippians 3:7-11**, where the apostle Paul describes the supreme greatness of knowing Jesus. And you can catch more passion for putting God first in **Psalm 63:1-8** and **Psalm 84**.

- Back in the Old Testament, God gave Moses his top Ten Command-ments etched on two stone tablets. And the command to put God first appears at the very top of those tablets. It says, "I am the Lord your God, who brought you out of Egypt, out of the land of slavery. *You shall have no other gods before me*" (**Exodus 20:2-3**, emphasis added).

- Read **Exodus 32:15-35** and notice this significant point: The Israelites melted their gold and made that golden calf the minute they stopped believing God cared for them. Keeping God first only makes sense when you are convinced he cares for you completely.

- Check out the rest of what Jesus said about possessions by reading **Matthew 6:19-34**. It's a key part of what's known as his "Sermon on the Mount."

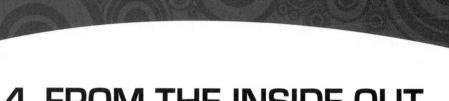

4. FROM THE INSIDE OUT

Follow because you want to

2 Corinthians 5:14 (NLT)

Either way, Christ's love controls us.

START The apostle Paul didn't let anything get in the way of his following Jesus. But believers in the ancient city of Corinth insulted him for his faith. Not only did they think they were more spiritual than Paul, but they also thought his sacrificial dedication to God was a little dense. Paul doesn't stand for their smartmouthing, and throughout his letters to the Corinthians he unleashes his reasons for his devotion to Christ. "You think I'm crazy?" he says. "You want to know why I'm so committed to God? Let me tell you."

What motivates you to follow God? Do you live as a Christian because you want to—or because something makes you feel you have to?

READ 2 Corinthians 5:14-15 (NLT)

> [14] Either way, Christ's love controls us. Since we believe that Christ died for all, we also believe that we have all died to the old life. [15] He died for everyone so that those who receive his new life will no longer live to please themselves. Instead, they will live for Christ, who died and was raised for them.

THINK Why does Paul do whatever he does?

How does Christ's love make a difference in how Paul lives?

The phrase "because Christ's love controls us" literally says "the love of Christ controls us." The phrase can mean that everything we do is motivated either by our love for Christ—or by Christ's love for us. Actually, it covers both.

Since Jesus died for everyone, we've all "died to" something. What is it? What does that mean?

Why did Jesus die and rise?

When you realize what Jesus has done by dying and rising for you, no one has to force you to live for him. You can follow him because you want to, not because you have to.

LIVE How often do you think about Christ's love for you? How much does it matter to your life as a Christian?

How would following Jesus be different if he used fear or brute force to motivate you?

Lots of Christians find their desire to live for God sometimes sputters or even stops at times. How can Christ's love help keep your faith strong and steady?

WRAP Your desire to follow God won't last if it's fueled by anything less than his boundless love for you. Jesus gave himself for you, dying in your place. He rose to prove that he rules the universe and that all his promises are true. So you can gladly let him lead your life and fill you with a passionate desire to live for him. Empowered by Christ's love, you'll soar to new heights.

» MORE THOUGHTS TO MULL

- This passage is a great summary of your relationship with God. Take the time to memorize all of 2 Corinthians 5:14-15.

- How have you been changed because you are a Christian? What have you died to?

- What people do you know who need the message of this passage? Share it with them.

» MORE SCRIPTURES TO DIG

- You can read more about the depths of the apostle Paul's devotion to Jesus in **2 Corinthians 11:16-33**, where Paul offers a list of all he's suffered for his faith, from stoning to shipwreck.

- Listen to what Jesus said about following him, in the fresh words of *The Message* paraphrase of the Bible: "Walk with me and work with me—watch how I do it. Learn the unforced rhythms of grace. I won't lay anything heavy or ill-fitting on you. Keep company with me and you'll learn to live freely and lightly" (**Matthew 11:29-30**).

- Read the larger context of Paul's words in **2 Corinthians 5:11-21**, where he says that anyone who believes in Jesus has become a new creation. God has made you a new person. Your old life is gone. Your new life has begun. You have been brought back to God. And God wants you to spread this "message of reconciliation" to others.

5. READY TO GO

Psalm 32:8 (NLT)

The Lord says, "I will guide you along the best pathway for your life. I will advise you and watch over you."

START God wants to lead you through life. But he doesn't map your route online or speak turn-by-turn directions via onboard GPS. His directions for your life aren't always as instant or obvious as the latest technology, but they're far more personal. And note that the closer you get to the end of high school, the closer you are to making some of the biggest decisions of your life, from your mission to your mate to whether you really want to follow God as your master. And getting God's guidance starts with believing he wants to give it.

How do you decide where you're headed in life?

READ Psalm 32:7-11 (NLT)

> [7] For you are my hiding place; you protect me from trouble. You surround me with songs of victory. [8] The Lord says, "I will guide you along the best pathway for your life. I will advise you and watch over you. [9] Do not be like a senseless horse or mule that needs a bit and bridle to keep it under control." [10] Many sorrows come to the wicked, but unfailing love surrounds those who trust the Lord. [11] So rejoice in the Lord and be glad, all you who obey him! Shout for joy, all you whose hearts are pure!

THINK That passage starts with words from the songwriter King David. What does he think of God?

When God speaks, what does he promise? What does he warn against?

That's an unforgettable picture not only of God's eagerness to guide you but also your need for his help. God doesn't want to drag you from place to place in his plan. And you don't want to be dragged.

David speaks up again in verses 10 and 11. What happens to people who rebel against God? What happens to those who trust and obey?

LIVE Do you believe the God of the universe knows you, grasps your situation, and wants to show you "the best pathway to your life"? Why—or why not?

Why would God want to guide the human race and especially you?

If you had to make a significant decision today—like choosing between going out for a sport or getting a part-time job—how would you involve God in that decision?

Do you think God wants to be part of all your decisions—or just the big ones? Why do you think that?

WRAP It might sound bizarre beyond imagination to claim that the God of the universe has a plan for your life. But God doesn't just have a plan for you, he promises to show you what it is. God is so ready to guide you that he compares you to a headstrong mule if you don't take him up on his offer. Remember Jeremiah 29:11? God has a good plan for your life—and he really doesn't want you to miss out.

» MORE THOUGHTS TO MULL

- When have you asked God to guide or help you? How did that turn out?

- Does this passage match your picture of God? Do you expect him to be this involved in your life—or more hands-off? Why do you think that?

- How do you think God communicates his plan for your life to you? That is, how do you expect him to guide you?

» MORE SCRIPTURES TO DIG

- God pays attention to the tiniest details in your world. Like Jesus said, "What is the price of two sparrows—one copper coin? But not a single sparrow can fall to the ground without your Father knowing it" (**Matthew 10:29**, NLT). He added, "the very hairs on your head are all numbered" (**Matthew 10:30**, NLT). Get it? God knows you and notices what goes on in your life.

- Check out **Proverbs 16:9**. It says, "In their hearts human beings plan their course, but the Lord establishes their steps." You might think you have things all figured out, but God truly rules your life.

- The New Testament talks about the plans God has for you, and it even sheds some light on what they look like. **Ephesians 2:1-10** is one of the Bible's grand statements of what it means to belong to God, describing how believers go from being dead in sin to alive in Jesus. The passage wraps up with this amazing statement: "For we are God's handiwork, created in Christ Jesus to do good works, which God prepared in advance for us to do."

6. STRAIGHT AHEAD

Get God's map for your life

Proverbs 3:5-6

Trust in the Lord with all your heart and lean not on your own understanding; in all your ways submit to him, and he will make your paths straight.

START So now you know that God sees the real you. He has amazing plans for your life. He wants you to keep him first at all times, following him because you want to and not because you have to. He promises to guide you. But there's still one major question. Are you willing to get with his plan?

How ready are you to run with God's plan for you? How willing are you to go with God as he leads you turn-by-turn through life?

READ Proverbs 3:1-8

[1] My son, do not forget my teaching, but keep my commands in your heart, [2] for they will prolong your life many years and bring you peace and prosperity. [3] Let love and faithfulness never leave you; bind them around your neck, write them on the tablet of your heart. [4] Then you will win favor and a good name in the sight of God and humankind. [5] Trust in the Lord with all your heart and lean not on your own understanding; [6] in all your ways submit to him, and he will make your paths straight. [7] Do not be wise in your own eyes; fear the Lord and shun evil. [8] This will bring health to your body and nourishment to your bones.

THINK What are you supposed to do with God's commands? What will following his instructions do for you?

What happens if you make love and faithfulness (or "loyalty and reliability") your highest priority?

What does it mean to "trust in the Lord with all your heart"? What does that have to do with the next point, "in all your ways submit to him"?

What does God promise if you trust and submit to him? What do you think that looks like in real life?

LIVE What does it mean to "lean on your own understanding" or "be wise in your own eyes"? What's so bad about that?

Neither of those phrases refers to shutting off your brain. God doesn't want you to cook up plans without him or brainstorm ways to do evil. You'll quickly veer off God's best path for you if you don't decide ahead of time to respect him and run from sin.

What holds you back from letting God lead your life? What's tough about that decision?

Suppose you trust God with all your heart and submit every bit of your life to obeying him. How do you expect your life to turn out?

God doesn't promise you a life without difficulties or hardship. Jesus said it bluntly: "In this world you will have trouble" (John 16:33). But God will guide you through whatever lies ahead. His plan won't always look the way you expect, but God's incredible promise is to lead you through decisions major and minor.

WRAP Like most of God's best gifts, his promise to lead you is like a gigantic package topped with a stupendous bow. But God didn't offer you this gift so you could just sit and stare at the pretty wrapping paper. The real fun begins when you open the present and put it to use.

» MORE THOUGHTS TO MULL

- Who do you know that tries hard to figure out and follow God's will for his or her life? What can you learn from that person?

- Do you believe that God's plan for your life is a gift? Do you ever worry that you won't like what's in the package?

- What do you like—or not—about trusting God to guide your life?

» MORE SCRIPTURES TO DIG

- If all this sounds like God promises you totally smooth sailing throughout life, keep reading further in this Bible chapter. **Proverbs 3:11-12** tells you "do not despise the Lord's discipline." And multiple other places in the Bible—including **Romans 5:3-5**, **James 1:2-4**, and **1 Peter 1:3-9**—tell you God's goal is to make you strong through troubles, not just remove you from them.

- God doesn't lay out a whole life plan all at once. Expect him to lead you one step at a time, giving you exactly what you need to know in the moment to make the right choices, whether large or small. Have a look at **James 4:13-17**.

7. ASK GOD

Discovering God's plan—start with prayer

James 1:5

If any of you lacks wisdom, you should ask God, who gives generously to all without finding fault, and it will be given to you.

START God's plan for your life has three parts. He has an *ultimate* will for you—that you be a Christian. He has a *universal* will—that you heed his commands that apply to everybody. And he has a *specific* will—that you discover his one-of-a-kind plan for you. You don't have to wonder about God's ultimate will and universal will, because he makes them brilliantly clear in the Bible. But if you want to discover his specific will for your nitty-gritty decisions, you'll need to do some searching. And you'll want to start by asking God for wisdom.

What's the biggest decision you face in the next six months? How will you make that choice?

READ James 1:2-8

> [2] Consider it pure joy, my brothers and sisters, whenever you face trials of many kinds, [3] because you know that the testing of your faith produces perseverance. [4] Let perseverance finish its work so that you may be mature and complete, not lacking anything. [5] If any of you lacks wisdom, you should ask God, who gives generously to all without finding fault, and it will be given to you. [6] But when you ask, you must believe and not doubt, because the one who doubts is like a wave of the sea, blown and tossed by the wind. [7] Those who doubt should not think they will receive anything from the Lord; [8] they are double-minded and unstable in all they do.

THINK God has a personalized plan for your life. But as this passage points out, God's plan doesn't always do away with difficulties. How are you supposed to react when you face a trial? Why?

A trial is anything that puts you to the test, everything from hardship to temptation to choosing what to do with your life. Perseverance is the ability to stand firm, staying on your feet in a storm. Becoming "mature and complete" means growing into everything God has planned for you.

What kind of help can God give? How do you get that support?

What is God's attitude toward you as he gives you wisdom?

God knows exactly what you face, and he gives wisdom "generously" and "without finding fault." Translation: He's happy to guide you. And he won't make you feel stupid.

There's something that can get in the way of getting guidance from God. What is it? Why is that a problem?

God wants to give wisdom to people who are listening. In Bible terms listening means being ready to obey even before you know what God wants you to do. Being "double-minded" means half your brain is saying "I want God's guidance!" while the other half says, "I want to do my own thing!" You're ready to receive God's wisdom when you expect him to guide you and you're excited to follow his leading.

LIVE Think of that big decision that looms in your next six months. What kind of specific wisdom do you need from God?

When you ask God for wisdom, how do you expect him to give it?

WRAP God wants to show you his specific will. And as you'll see in the next three studies, he uses a variety of means to direct you—including the Bible, circumstances, and wise advice. But the process starts with prayer. If you lay out your needs, God will figure out how to show you his way.

» MORE THOUGHTS TO MULL

- What's the difference between God's ultimate will, universal will, and specific will?

- Sum it up in your own words: What does prayer have to do with discovering God's specific will?

- Talk to God about some areas where you need guidance, now and down the road.

» MORE SCRIPTURES TO DIG

- God wants you to be "mature and complete" like Jesus—what the Bible calls "conformed to the image of his Son." Read **Romans 8:28-30** to see how he uses all the happenings of your life to get you to this goal.

- It might be tough to believe God hears you when you pray about your real-life concerns, especially if your issues feel small. Check out the model prayer Jesus taught his closest followers in **Matthew 6:5-13**. You'll see that "the Lord's Prayer" covers the whole range of life, from your daily food to the glory of the Almighty God. And flip through the book of **Psalms** to see that you can talk to God about anything.

- Look at **Matthew 7:7** for an amazing verse about asking God for what you need. Jesus said, "Ask and it will be given to you; seek and you will find; knock and the door will be opened to you." But don't take that as a blanket promise that God will give you whatever you ask for, no questions asked. Why? Because God only gives you his best. He doesn't grant requests that go against his will. Like the Bible says elsewhere, "This is the confidence we have in approaching God: that if we ask anything according to his will, he hears us. And if we know that he hears us—whatever we ask—we know that we have what we asked of him" (**1 John 5:14-15**).

8. READ THE MANUAL

Psalm 119:10

I seek you with all my heart; do not let me stray from your commands.

START If the Bible were just another book of ancient literature, you could glance past it and let it gather dust. But since the Bible is God's Word, you would be wise to let it lead your life. Not only does it show you "salvation through faith in Christ Jesus," but it's also "useful for teaching, for showing people what is wrong in their lives, for correcting faults, and for teaching how to live right" (2 Timothy 3:16, NCV). The Bible is a great place to get wisdom from the all-knowing God. It's where you start to discover his plan for you.

How have you used the Bible to figure out your life? If you haven't—why not?

READ Psalm 119:1-5, 9-11

> [1] Blessed are those whose ways are blameless, who walk according to the law of the Lord. [2] Blessed are those who keep his statutes and seek him with all their heart—[3] they do no wrong but follow his ways. [4] You have laid down precepts that are to be fully obeyed. [5] Oh, that my ways were steadfast in obeying your decrees! [9] How can those who are young keep their way pure? By living according to your word. [10] I seek you with all my heart; do not let me stray from your commands. [11] I have hidden your word in my heart that I might not sin against you.

THINK To be "blessed" means to be "fortunate" or even "happy." It's experiencing God's favor and joy. Who in this passage is blessed?

The New Testament says that none of us can keep God's commands perfectly, so Jesus came to die for our sins and make us right with God (Romans 3:21-26). But the principal in this passage still holds true. If we ignore God's commands, we won't experience his kind of happiness. If we continually break his rules, brokenness will rule our lives.

How can the Bible keep your life on the right path?

Psalm 119:105 declares, "Your word is a lamp to my feet and a light for my path." As you study the Bible, you quickly spot God's universal will, the commands he intends for all believers to follow—commands that tell you his plan for almost every part of life. You don't have to wonder, for example, if God wants you to be sexually pure (1 Thessalonians 4:3) or obey your parents (Ephesians 6:1-3). God also uses the Bible to communicate his specific will for you. But you won't catch his detailed guidance if you're ignoring these big commands.

LIVE There's not a chapter and verse in the Bible that tells you whether you should go to college or get a job. It doesn't say whether the spouse you choose should have brown eyes or blue. But have you ever sensed God speaking to you through the Bible—like right to YOU?

Sometimes as you read the Bible, it's as if the words jump off the page. Sometimes it seems like they might reach up and slap you. That can be the Holy Spirit nudging you to listen hard and apply a truth to your situation. It's why the Bible is "alive and active" (Hebrews 4:12), not dead and dusty like other ancient books. It's also how God can use the Bible to show you his specific will for you.

How can you make reading the Bible a regular habit? If you're already there, what got you to that point?

How could you listen better to God speaking to you—and guiding you—through the Bible?

Do you think the Bible is a reliable guide to life in your real world? Why—or why not?

WRAP God makes his infinite wisdom known in the pages of Scripture. If you want him to guide you, get into his Word and let him teach you about your world—and about you. The Bible is your instruction manual for life.

» MORE THOUGHTS TO MULL

- Is reading the Bible easy or hard for you? Is it interesting or boring? Why?

- Name someone you know who looks to the Bible for guidance in life. Why does that person trust the Bible?

- It's one thing to read the Bible and another to remember it. Make a plan to memorize the verse at the start of each study in *Soar*.

» MORE SCRIPTURES TO DIG

- **Psalm 119** is the longest chapter in the Bible, and it happens to be all about the greatness of God's words. Give it a read. **Psalm 19** is like a miniature version of Psalm 119. Read it too.

- The Bible teaches that God speaks to us through his work of creation, teaching us enough about himself that we are "without excuse." We can tell that God put us here, that we belong to him, and that we answer to him (**Romans 1:19-20**). But God has also spoken in words, first through his prophets (**2 Peter 1:19-22**) and then through Jesus, whom the Bible says is the Word, God fully on display (**John 1:1-14**). The Bible wraps together all of God's words for you to read firsthand. More than any other source of knowledge, the Bible tells you how to find God and live for him.

- This book keeps you busy reading the Bible—for now. If you're not sure where to read in the Bible on your own, check out these prime Bible books: **Mark** (a fast read about the facts about Jesus), **John** (a panoramic view of Jesus the Savior), **Philippians** (a joyful letter from the apostle Paul to some of his best friends), or **Ephesians** (a good mix of deep thoughts about God and practical tips for living).

9. LISTEN UP

Proverbs 4:4-5

Take hold of my words with all
your heart; keep my commands,
and you will live. Get wisdom, get
understanding; do not forget my
words or turn away from them.

START Maybe you've got an older sibling or friend who feeds you solid advice. Or a group of peers that steers you straight time after time. Or parents, pastors, teachers, coaches, and bosses you can truly count on. But you might also be getting so-called facts about life shoveled at you from people who aren't so smart. God wants to surround you with people whose words lift you up and make you soar. Like Proverbs 15:22 says, "Plans fail for lack of counsel, but with many advisers they succeed."

Who do you trust to give you the advice you need to succeed?

READ Proverbs 4:1-7, 10-13

> ¹ Listen, my sons, to a father's instruction; pay attention and gain understanding. ² I give you sound learning, so do not forsake my teaching. ³ For I too was a son to my father, still tender, and cherished by my mother. ⁴ Then he taught me, and he said to me, "Take hold of my words with all your heart; keep my commands, and you will live. ⁵ Get wisdom, get understanding; do not forget my words or turn away from them. ⁶ Do not forsake wisdom, and she will protect you; love her, and she will watch over you. ⁷ The beginning of wisdom is this: Get wisdom. Though it cost all you have, get understanding. ¹⁰ Listen, my son, accept what I say, and the years of your life will be many. ¹¹ I instruct you in the way of wisdom and lead you along straight paths. ¹² When you walk, your steps will not be hampered; when you run, you will not stumble. ¹³ Hold on to instruction, do not let it go; guard it well, for it is your life.

THINK Why listen to your father and mother?

Not only do your parents probably know you better than anyone else does, they've been around the block once. Or twice. Yet the father in this passage warns his children not to reject his counsel. Why is it tempting to ignore parental input?

Why does this father mention that he was once a kid? Does that point persuade you?

If you give wisdom a chance, what all will it do for you?

LIVE Honestly, are you usually more of a wisdom-seeker—or a wisdom-shunning fool? Why?

When have you sought out someone for advice? What was tough about that? What made it worth the effort?

God specifically gives parents the task of imparting wisdom to their children. He says, "Start children off on the way they should go, and even when they are old they will not turn from it" (Proverbs 22:6). How quick are you to accept direction from your parents?

Why do you think God chooses to use people as one way he guides you?

WRAP God doesn't leave you alone to figure out his will all by yourself. He wants you to realize he is the source of all wisdom. He wants to speak to you through Scripture. But he also uses the people in your life to help you know the right path.

» MORE THOUGHTS TO MULL

- Why do some people choose to go it alone rather than seeking advice from others?

- What's the downside of looking to others for wisdom? Is it possible to depend too much on others? Give some examples.

- When would you go against the advice of people who know you well and have your best interests in mind?

» MORE SCRIPTURES TO DIG

- The Bible is packed with wisdom to help you find your way in life. While it's not the same as hearing from people around you, the Bible offers time-tested, God-given insights for every facet of life. Read **Proverbs 1** for descriptions of wisdom and foolishness.

- Solomon is the best-known wisdom writer of the Bible, remembered as the author of 3,000 proverbs. He was famous throughout the known world for his insights, and he's best known for the good judgment he displayed in **1 Kings 3:16-28**, where he proposed slicing a baby in half to discover the child's real mother. Read more about Solomon in **1 Kings 4:29-34, 10:1-29**.

- Five Old Testament books are classified as "wisdom literature," storehouses of practical and spiritual insight for life and love—Job, Psalms, Proverbs, Ecclesiastes, and Song of Solomon. It's easy to jump in and read a few verses at a time anywhere in **Proverbs**, while **Ecclesiastes** has pushed countless generations to ponder the meaning of life.

10. OPEN AND SHUT

Discovering God's plan–read circumstances

2 Corinthians 2:12

...I went to Troas to preach the gospel of Christ and found that the Lord had opened a door for me....

START God doesn't just guide you through prayer, the Bible, and solid advice. Sometimes he shows you where to go and what to do—or not—through circumstances. At times the apostle Paul recognized God at work in a situation, opening a door of opportunity for him. At other times he saw God shaping circumstances by closing a door, blocking him from pursuing a certain path. In both "open" and "shut" doors, Paul noticed God's guiding hand.

When have circumstances forced your life to go one way or the other? How did you see God in that—or not?

READ 2 Corinthians 2:12-13

> [12] Now when I went to Troas to preach the gospel of Christ and found that the Lord had opened a door for me, [13] I still had no peace of mind, because I did not find my brother Titus there. So I said goodby to them and went on to Macedonia.

THINK Paul went to preach in Troas, a city in the northwest corner of what is now Turkey. Titus was Paul's spiritual brother, a younger partner for whom the New Testament letter "Titus" is named. When Paul didn't find Titus in Troas, he crossed the Aegean Sea to Macedonia, in modern Greece.

God had opened a door for Paul to preach in Troas. What did Paul do with that opportunity?

LIVE When have you encountered an obviously "shut" door? When have you found an "open" door?

If God had opened the door for Paul to preach, shouldn't he have stayed in Troas? Why—or why not?

Here's where interpreting circumstances gets tricky. Paul, for example, found an opportunity in Troas, likely preaching there enough to realize he had a crowd of responsive listeners. But he was concerned for Titus and went looking for him. You might face that same kind of decision. You can have an open door in front of you. Maybe multiple, wonderful open doors. But that doesn't mean you're automatically supposed to walk through them or stay there forever. Figuring out your next step still takes time, prayer, and wise advice from others.

Suppose Paul had gone to Troas and found a tough crowd unwilling to listen to him. Should he have stayed and preached? Why—or why not?

Again, how to read your circumstances isn't always immediately clear. You might want to do something that feels impossible. Give it a try! After all you know that God doesn't want you to give up because of difficulties. He might want you to keep knocking until the door opens. And you can keep asking him for clarity.

When have you pushed on a door that seemed shut—and gotten through?

When have you banged hard on a door you really wanted to be open—but still got stopped?

How can you tell if a "shut" door is really shut—or an "open" door is really open?

WRAP Discovering God's will doesn't happen in an instant. You start with prayer, the Bible, and good counsel. Then you add circumstances to the mix, knowing they can be tough to interpret. God, after all, might want you to learn persistence—or patience. But hang on to God's promise: Trust in him, and he will make your path straight.

» MORE THOUGHTS TO MULL

- You've heard about using prayer, Scripture, advice, and circumstances to discover God's plans for you. Does this make sense—or not? Who can help you figure it out?

- Think back to that big decision you need to make in the next six months. Given what you know, how are you going to make that choice?

- Learning to spot God's will for your life means you need to stick close to him. Suppose God sent you a text each day telling you exactly what to do. How would that change your relationship for the better—or worse?

» MORE SCRIPTURES TO DIG

- Paul alludes to a shut door in **Romans 1:13**. Paul mentions an open door again in **Colossians 4:2-4**. He wrote, "Devote yourselves to prayer, being watchful and thankful. And pray for us, too, that God may open a door for our message, so that we may proclaim the mystery of Christ, for which I am in chains. Pray that I may proclaim it clearly, as I should."

- Read more in **1 Peter 1:6-9** about God developing your ability to persevere.

11. YOU CHOOSE!

Do right and do what you want

Psalm 37:4

Take delight in the Lord and he will give you the desires of your heart.

START The Bible is clear that God wants to show you his will, his step-by-step plan for your life. But what should you do when you've prayed, dug into the Bible, searched out advice, and thought hard about your circumstances—yet God hasn't shown you an answer? Maybe you need to wait on God a bit longer. But what if you reach a point where you have no choice but to choose? Then God seems to be saying, "Do what you want!"

Have you ever asked God to show you what to do or how to figure out a problem, but he seemed silent? What did you do?

READ Psalm 37:1-6

> ¹ Do not fret because of those who are evil or be envious of those who do wrong; ² for like the grass they will soon wither, like green plants they will soon die away. ³ Trust in the Lord and do good; dwell in the land and enjoy safe pasture. ⁴ Take delight in the Lord and he will give you the desires of your heart. ⁵ Commit your way to the Lord; trust in him and he will do this: ⁶ He will make your righteous reward shine like the dawn, your vindication like the noonday sun.

THINK The world is full of people who do wrong and do well because of it. Why shouldn't you worry about them?

Now comes the big point. While all those people are doing whatever it takes to get ahead, how should you do life?

This psalm gives you some of God's most basic rules for living: Trust him, do good, stick close to him, and count on him for your protection and provision. If you do those things, you won't wander from God's path for your life. But there's more. If you "delight in the Lord," what will God do for you?

The first half of verse 4 isn't a catch, but it is a condition. When you recognize God as your loving master and put him first in your life, your heart will begin to want what he wants. So when you can't see the details of his specific will for you, then you're free to follow the best choice your heart and head can make. God is leaving the decision up to you. He's saying, "You choose!"

What does God promise to do when you commit your whole life to him?

LIVE Suppose you decide to totally follow God, obeying him in every way you know. What would that be like?

Why do you think God sometimes leaves choices—even big choices—up to you?

By now you've probably caught the point that God doesn't always send an immediate, unmistakable answer every time you ask him for advice. Are you okay with that? Why—or why not?

WRAP God isn't satisfied with just handing you answers to your prayers for guidance. He wants to lead you step-by-step, talking with you often and interacting in a real relationship. Why? Because his friendship with you is even more important than his plan for your life.

» MORE THOUGHTS TO MULL

- Have you ever simply prayed, "God, I want you—and I want all of your will in my life"? Try it. Watch what happens.

- What about following God's plans doesn't sound like a good idea?

- Are you confident in your ability to make good decisions when God seems to leave the choice up to you? Explain your answer.

» MORE SCRIPTURES TO DIG

- Go back to where you started in this book. **Jeremiah 29:11** leaves no doubt how good it is to follow God's map for your life: "For I know the plans I have for you," declares the Lord, "plans to prosper you and not to harm you, plans to give you hope and a future." Can you see now that God really does have good plans for you? Do you understand how he wants to communicate them to you?

- Christians talk a lot about God wanting to lead and control us. But God never bypasses your brain or your heart in leading you through life. In fact self-control is one of the major qualities God wants to grow in you. Self-control is a fruit of the Spirit (**Galatians 5:22-23**). A lack of self-control leads to all kinds of evil (**2 Timothy 3:2-5**). Self-control is the next step after you gain knowledge of what God wants you to do (**2 Peter 1:6**). But self-control is the opposite of timidity, which suggests a fear of life that has nothing do with the confidence we can have in God (**2 Timothy 1:7**).

- Don't miss other amazing parts of this psalm. Look at Psalm **37:23-26** and **37:37-40**.

12. USE THEM OR LOSE THEM

How to invest your talents

Matthew 25:21

His master replied, "Well done, good and faithful servant! You have been faithful with a few things; I will put you in charge of many things. Come and share your master's happiness!"

START You probably don't expect to become a billionaire, even in your craziest dreams. But the Bible says that God has already loaded you up with priceless gifts, including the biggest gift of all—the total package called *you*.

What talents and abilities has God given you? How do you plan to put them to use?

READ Matthew 25:14-21

[14] "Again, it will be like a man going on a journey, who called his servants and entrusted his wealth to them. [15] To one he gave five bags of gold, to another two bags, and to another one bag, each according to his ability. Then he went on his journey. [16] The man who had received five bags of gold went at once and put his money to work and gained five bags more. [17] So also, the one with two bags of gold gained two more. [18] But the man who had received one bag went off, dug a hole in the ground and hid his master's money. [19] After a long time the master of those servants returned and settled accounts with them. [20] The man who had received five bags of gold brought the other five. 'Master,' he said, 'you entrusted me with five bags of gold. See, I have gained five more.' [21] His master replied, 'Well done, good and faithful servant! You have been faithful with a few things; I will put you in charge of many things. Come and share your master's happiness!'"

THINK Don't feel sorry for the guy who got "only" a single bag of gold, because the master trusted each servant with astronomical sums. Each bag was worth about 20 years' salary. Jesus told this parable, by the way, as part of his teaching on his coming again to earth. He was talking about what in life is truly important.

What did the men with five and two bags of gold do with their money?

What did the guy entrusted with one bag do?

How did the master react to the servant with five bags of gold, who doubled his master's money?

If you were to grab a Bible and read the rest of this story, you'd find that the guy who was given two bags and doubled them also received a joyful response from the master. (Matthew 25:22-26). But what about the guy who buried his money in a hole and made no profit—what reaction do you think he got?

That answer isn't too tough to guess, but here are the details. The master calls him "wicked" and "lazy," takes his lone bag and gives it to the guy who already has ten, and tosses the man into the darkness, "where there will be weeping and gnashing of teeth" (Matthew 25:26-30).

LIVE Why would a master—or God—be so angry if you didn't use what he entrusted to you?

Paul once asked the Corinthians, "What do you have that you did not receive?" (1 Corinthians 4:7). In other words everything you have is a gift from God, including talents, abilities, spiritual insight, family support, money, hobbies, interests, personality, and spiritual gifts. He wants you to use those gifts to honor him and show his love to your world. If you don't use your gifts, the world goes without.

What will the world miss out on if you keep your gifts to yourself?

WRAP God has given you vast riches, a lifetime of time and talents. The most important thing you can do with your life is to use the gifts he has entrusted to you, giving back what he's already given you. So how much do you have? What do you have? How can you wisely invest your life to serve God? You have a lifetime to figure it out, and there's never a better time to start than right now. It's all part of the fun.

» MORE THOUGHTS TO MULL

- Why not use your gifts for your own benefit?

- How are you using your gifts for God—or not? What opportunities exist at school, at church, and around your home?

- Do the math and figure out how many seconds you have in your life to serve God. That's at least one way you'll likely be a billionaire. Spend all those seconds wisely.

» MORE SCRIPTURES TO DIG

- Using your gifts to honor God and love your world isn't limited to Sundays or special times you set aside to serve. It's an attitude you can take with you wherever you go. The apostle Paul put it simply: "So whether you eat or drink or whatever you do, do it all for the glory of God" (**1 Corinthians 10:31**).

- **Matthew 25:31-46** offers a stunning example of using your gifts to serve God in everyday ways. Jesus applauds a group that had fed the hungry, clothed the naked, visited the imprisoned, and hung out with strangers and the sick. Serving others had become so natural to these people that they didn't recognize they had done amazing things, actually ministering to Jesus himself as they ministered to others.

- Read **1 Corinthians 12** and **14** to learn about the special spiritual gifts God has built inside you. More on those in the next study.

13. GIFTED BY GOD

Put your spiritual gifts to work

1 Corinthians 12:7

Now to each one the manifestation of the Spirit is given for the common good.

START Some of the spiritual gifts discussed in this next Bible passage look very everydayish. Others are mindblowingly spectacular. A few cause gigantic controversy. But the point of the passage is that God has given each Christian special gifts to show off God's goodness, exclaim his greatness, and proclaim the Good News of Jesus' death and resurrection—all so that God's kingdom is built up.

What do you know about spiritual gifts? What are they?

READ 1 Corinthians 12:1, 4-11

> [1] Now about the gifts of the Spirit, brothers and sisters, I do not want you to be uninformed. [4] There are different kinds of gifts, but the same Spirit distributes them. [5] There are different kinds of service, but the same Lord. [6] There are different kinds of working, but in all of them and in everyone it is the same God at work. [7] Now to each one the manifestation of the Spirit is given for the common good. [8] To one there is given through the Spirit a message of wisdom, to another a message of knowledge by means of the same Spirit, [9] to another faith by the same Spirit, to another gifts of healing by that one Spirit, [10] to another miraculous powers, to another prophecy, to another distinguishing between spirits, to another speaking in different kinds of tongues, and to still another the interpretation of tongues. [11] All these are the work of one and the same Spirit, and he distributes them to each one, just as he determines.

THINK The apostle Paul gets right to the point. He doesn't want you to go through life knowing nothing about gifts of the Spirit. Jot down the gifts listed here.

This is one Bible list of spiritual gifts. There are other gift catalogs in 1 Corinthians 14:1-30, Ephesians 4:11-13, and Romans 12:4-8. The point of each list is that each of the many different abilities is uniquely valuable and absolutely necessary.

So does God skip anyone when he passes out spiritual gifts to Christians?

What are you supposed to do with your gift? Whom is it supposed to benefit?

LIVE What gifts has God given you—not just spiritual gifts, but all sorts? What are you good at?

Do you ever get jealous and wish you had someone else's assortment of gifts?

How can you use the qualities that make you uniquely you to build up the people around you and pull them closer to God?

How will your world be different if you use your gifts? What will the world lack if you don't?

WRAP God doesn't give dumb gifts. Next to Jesus the biggest gift you can give your friends is *you*. As American poet e.e. cummings wrote, "The hardest battle is to be nobody but yourself in a world which is doing its best, night and day, to make you everybody else."

» MORE THOUGHTS TO MULL

- What is your first reaction when you look at this list of spiritual gifts—or the other lists in 1 Corinthians 14, Ephesians 4, and Romans 12?

- Who in your immediate world understands spiritual gifts? Since God says he's definitely given you a spiritual gift, who can help you develop that special ability?

- Want to learn more about identifying and appreciating your incredible giftedness? Grab a copy *Find Your Fit*, a book I cowrote with human resources expert Jane Kise. You'll never look down on yourself again.

» MORE SCRIPTURES TO DIG

- Spiritual gifts are only one part of the package of God's gifts to you. Look at the apostle Paul, for example. He had the spiritual gift of apostleship (**Romans 1:1**), which is the ability to lead multiple churches and to declare the Good News across cultures. He also had a talent for tent making, which determined where he would preach (**Acts 18:1-4**). He had a personality unafraid of conflict (**Galatians 2:1-15**). And he had a passion to preach where no one else had preached before (**2 Corinthians 10:16**). You too have a great mix of gifts inside you.

- **Galatians 6:4** says to keep your eyes on your own actions—and take pride in yourself, not comparing yourself to others.

- You've got to take a look at **1 Corinthians 12:14-26**, where Paul does a comic riff on how all our different gifts work together in the church, just like the parts of the body.

14. MORE STUFF

Put everything in its right place

1 Timothy 6:6

But godliness with contentment is great gain.

START Jesus expects to rule over your whole life, both now and in every moment of your future. And back in study 3 you already heard that material things can easily push him out of the top spot. Even Christians get caught up in making life all about getting bigger and better stuff. They join the clubs, do the sports, hang with the right people, pick an impressive college, build a stellar résumé, and aim for the best job—all so they can shop, travel, build, and consume. Like the Bible says, they "fall into temptation and a trap" (1 Timothy 6:9).

How many of your future dreams focus on obtaining the things and experiences money can buy?

READ 1 Timothy 6:6-12

> [6] But godliness with contentment is great gain. [7] For we brought nothing into the world, and we can take nothing out of it. [8] But if we have food and clothing, we will be content with that. [9] Those who want to get rich fall into temptation and a trap and into many foolish and harmful desires that plunge people into ruin and destruction. [10] For the love of money is a root of all kinds of evil. Some people, eager for money, have wandered from the faith and pierced themselves with many griefs. [11] But you, man of God, flee from all this, and pursue righteousness, godliness, faith, love, endurance and gentleness. [12] Fight the good fight of the faith. Take hold of the eternal life to which you were called when you made your good confession in the presence of many witnesses.

THINK You probably have a detailed mental picture of what "rich" looks like—and why it's good. But the apostle Paul tells his young friend Timothy that something else is "great wealth." What is it? Explain in your own words what that thing is.

"Contentment" means being "satisfied" or "at ease." Why is being content with the basics (like "food and clothing") a good idea? What happens to people "who want to get rich" and are "eager for money"?

This passage offers an alternative to chasing wealth. What better things can you do with your life?

LIVE Do you think you're rich? Is this passage for you or for someone else? Explain.

How have you seen people get hurt by a desire to get rich? How has it impacted their families, friends, faith, etc.?

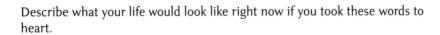

Describe what your life would look like right now if you took these words to heart.

How could living out this passage transform your long-term life plans?

WRAP Having a comfortable life tops the concerns of most people, both for right now and the rest of life. But when the love of money drives you, Jesus ends up in the back seat...or the trunk...or maybe left in the dust. That's not part of God's plan for you.

» MORE THOUGHTS TO MULL

- Agree or disagree: It's impossible to enthusiastically pursue both God and money.

- Suppose you decide your plans for life shouldn't revolve around accumulating stuff. What else could you do with a lifetime of time, money, and energy? What causes could you commit yourself to?

- Do you know anyone who keeps money in proper perspective? What can you learn from that person?

» MORE SCRIPTURES TO DIG

- You've heard how Jesus said to seek God's kingdom above anything else (**Matthew 6:33**). In that same message he made some pointed remarks about money. Here's one that has everything to do with your plans for life: "No one can serve two masters. Either you will hate the one and love the other, or you will be devoted to the one and despise the other. You cannot serve both God and money" (**Matthew 6:24**).

- The apostle Paul penned the Bible's best-ever statement on contentment. Look at what he wrote to the Christians in Philippi: "I have learned to be content whatever the circumstances. I know what it is to be in need, and I know what it is to have plenty. I have learned the secret of being content in any and every situation, whether well fed or hungry, whether living in plenty or in want. I can do all this through him who gives me strength" (**Philippians 4:11-13**).

- Here's one more wise word on money. Agur son of Jakeh prays: "Give me neither poverty nor riches, but give me only my daily bread. Otherwise, I may have too much and disown you and say, 'Who is the Lord?' Or I may become poor and steal, and so dishonor the name of my God" (**Proverbs 30:8-9**).

15. CHEERFUL GIVER

Live generously

2 Corinthians 9:7

Each of you should give what you have decided in your heart to give, not reluctantly or under compulsion, for God loves a cheerful giver.

START Sure, the Bible says the love of money is the source of all kinds of evil (1 Timothy 6:10). But that's not the whole story. While abusing money can cause major destruction, using money well can do massive good. Like the apostle Paul said, "Command those who are rich in this present world not to be arrogant nor to put their hope in wealth, which is so uncertain, but to put their hope in God, who richly provides us with everything for our enjoyment. Command them to do good, to be rich in good deeds, and to be generous and willing to share" (1 Timothy 6:17-18).

When have you seen money used for good?

READ 2 Corinthians 9:6-11

> [6] Remember this: Whoever sows sparingly will also reap sparingly, and whoever sows generously will also reap generously. [7] Each of you should give what you have decided in your heart to give, not reluctantly or under compulsion, for God loves a cheerful giver. [8] And God is able to bless you abundantly, so that in all things at all times, having all that you need, you will abound in every good work. [9] As it is written: "They have scattered abroad their gifts to the poor; their righteousness endures forever." [10] Now he who supplies seed to the sower and bread for food will also supply and increase your store of seed and will enlarge the harvest of your righteousness. [11] You will be made rich in every way so that you can be generous on every occasion, and through us your generosity will result in thanksgiving to God.

THINK In this letter to the church at Corinth, the apostle Paul starts with a picture from farming. To "sow" means to plant seed in the ground, while to "reap" means to harvest the mature plants. What happens if you "sow sparingly"? What if you "sow generously"? When have you seen that principle at work in real life?

List three facts from this passage about how God wants you to give.

Look at verses 8-11. Why does God want to bless people who give abundantly? What all will he do?

LIVE When have you given money—or time or energy—and felt good about it? When have you felt like it was a waste?

If you were surprised that God wants you to be content with the basics, you might be shocked that he wants you to give both cheerfully and generously. How good are you at giving cheerfully? How about generously?

Do you think God sounds greedy—like he just wants your money?

Actually, God doesn't sound much like television preachers who want to get your money by turning you upside down and shaking you by the ankles. God reminded his Old Testament people that "every animal of the forest is mine, and the cattle on a thousand hills" (Psalm 50:10), so he wasn't after offerings. What he really wants is your heart. And he wants you to enjoy the privilege of helping others.

How can you make generous giving a part of your present and future plans?

WRAP It's easy to think your stuff belongs to you. But everything you are and own actually belongs to God. And you can't miss the fact that his plan for you is to share.

» MORE THOUGHTS TO MULL

- How does giving to others prevent money from becoming your god?

- Jesus said, "It is more blessed to give than to receive" (Acts 20:35). Do you agree with him? Why—or why not?

- Growing in generosity is usually a little-by-little thing. What next step can you take to be a glad giver?

» MORE SCRIPTURES TO DIG

- Dig into the background of this passage by reading **2 Corinthians 8:1-5**. Paul wanted his readers in Corinth to support believers in Macedonia, who were "in the midst of a very severe trial" and experiencing "extreme poverty." Paul also applauded the Macedonians for giving generously even when they had little.

- You might doubt that anything you give has real impact. But check out these words from Paul. They're a big thank you—both from God and the people who benefit from your giving: "This service that you perform is not only supplying the needs of the Lord's people but is also overflowing in many expressions of thanks to God. Because of the service by which you have proved yourselves, people will praise God for the obedience that accompanies your confession of the gospel of Christ, and for your generosity in sharing with them and with everyone else. And in their prayers for you their hearts will go out to you, because of the surpassing grace God has given you. Thanks be to God for his indescribable gift!" (**2 Corinthians 9:12-15**).

16. STAND

1 Peter 5:8-9

Be alert and of sober mind. Your enemy the devil prowls around like a roaring lion looking for someone to devour. Resist him, standing firm in the faith.

START God wants nothing more than for you to stick close to him by following his plan for every step of your life. But not everyone who hears about your intention will be thrilled. In fact, whenever you decide to follow God wholeheartedly, you can expect opposition.

Who supports your decision to live as a Christian? Who ignores you, clashes with you, or makes you feel like a total idiot? What do they do?

READ 1 Peter 5:8-11

8 Be alert and of sober mind. Your enemy the devil prowls around like a roaring lion looking for someone to devour. 9 Resist him, standing firm in the faith, because you know that your fellow believers throughout the world are undergoing the same kind of sufferings. 10 And the God of all grace, who called you to his eternal glory in Christ, after you have suffered a little while, will himself restore you and make you strong, firm and steadfast. 11 To him be the power for ever and ever. Amen.

THINK The apostle Peter was writing to Christians across what is now Turkey. These believers were having a tough time living for God in a culture that didn't know him. They were misunderstood and cruelly persecuted. Why does Peter tell them to stay "alert" and "sober minded"?

Peter's readers knew they faced human opposition. Peter told them they also faced something even more sinister. What does the Devil want to do to them?

How can these suffering Christians get through their ordeal? Who else faces the same difficulties?

Not only do Christians "all over the world" today experience this spiritual opposition, so have Christians throughout time. But the God of grace, glory, and power won't let you get knocked around forever. He will pick you up and make you strong and steady.

LIVE Why do non-Christians sometimes make life miserable for Christians?

What do you think of the idea that the Devil wants to do you in?

How can you stay strong in your faith when you encounter opposition?

Look no further than Jesus himself for a picture of how to stay strong. Near the start of his ministry, Jesus experienced fierce opposition from the Devil himself—a series of temptations meant to disrupt the Father's plan that Jesus go to the cross and die for the world's sins. Jesus fought back by hanging tight to God's Word, quoting Scriptures that reassured his heart and silenced the Devil. Catch the scene in Matthew 4:1-11.

How can you get support from other Christians facing the same problems you do?

WRAP Don't ever assume that following God's plan for your life means you won't encounter problems. You will. But no matter what you have to endure, you will prevail.

» MORE THOUGHTS TO MULL

- How can opposition strengthen your commitment to follow God's plans for your life?

- When have you changed your behavior to avoid standing out as a Christian?

- How can Christians help one another stay strong?

» MORE SCRIPTURES TO DIG

- Bible scholars argue about exactly what challenges Peter's readers are facing. We can see in **1 Peter 3:8-17** and **4:12-19** that they were suffering for doing right. We also know that deadly action against Christians is only a year or two away in Rome, where Peter is likely living as he writes (**1 Peter 5:13**).

- Don't miss these encouraging words from earlier in the same chapter: "Humble yourselves, therefore, under God's mighty hand, that he may lift you up in due time. Cast all your anxiety on him because he cares for you" (**1 Peter 5:6-7**). When you suffer for your faith, you can be sure God has your back.

- Want a tight description of how you and your Christian friends can support one another? Try this: "Let us hold tightly without wavering to the hope we affirm, for God can be trusted to keep his promise. Let us think of ways to motivate one another to acts of love and good works. And let us not neglect our meeting together, as some people do, but encourage one another, especially now that the day of his return is drawing near" (**Hebrews 10:23-25,** NLT).

17. FAST AND STRONG

Run hard toward your goal

1 Corinthians 9:24

Do you not know that in a race
all the runners run, but only one
gets the prize? Run in such a way
as to get the prize.

START Like their Olympic-loving neighbors in Athens, the ancient Corinthians hosted their own premier athletic event; a multisport competition held every other year for centuries. When the apostle Paul wrote to Christians living in this city of fans wild about the Isthmian games, he grabbed the opportunity to make a major point about following Jesus.

Has there ever been a time you wanted to quit following Jesus? Describe your toughest episode or ongoing experience as a Christian.

READ 1 Corinthians 9:24-27

> [24] Do you not know that in a race all the runners run, but only one gets the prize? Run in such a way as to get the prize. [25] Everyone who competes in the games goes into strict training. They do it to get a crown that will not last; but we do it to get a crown that will last forever. [26] Therefore I do not run like someone running aimlessly; I do not fight like a boxer beating the air. [27] No, I strike a blow to my body and make it my slave so that after I have preached to others, I myself will not be disqualified for the prize.

THINK Paul starts with a fact known by every fan: Although many competitors enter a race, only one wins. And no one wins by being lazy. So what point is Paul making for believers?

What reward do race winners get? Why does Paul downplay that prize?

That "crown that will not last" awarded to winners was actually a wreath made of laurel or celery that quickly wilted. What reward does the Christian get? Why is that better?

How seriously does Paul train as a Christian? What all does he do?

Not only is Paul like a runner determined to stay on course, but he also resembles a boxer who disciplines his whole being into submission.

LIVE Sooner or later most believers endure outside opposition. But there's an inner fight Christians also experience, a battle with yourself to stay on track spiritually. What can you do to stay enthusiastic about God's plans for your life?

How do you discipline yourself to grow stronger in your Christian faith?

Why is it worth the effort to work hard and stay committed and focused as a Christian?

What one thing do you plan to do today to keep on track with God?

WRAP You don't have to be a world-class athlete to get Paul's point. Each of us chases all kinds of good goals. But if we neglect God's bigger purposes for us, the outcome will amount to a crown of drooping vegetables.

≫   MORE THOUGHTS TO MULL

- Does Paul's intense image of a runner or a boxer make sense to you as a metaphor for the Christian life? Why—or why not?

- Compared to all your other interests and activities, how much effort do you put into your Christian faith? And how do you see your Christian faith connecting to those other activities?

- When have you chased a goal or prize that in hindsight felt like wilted celery?

≫   MORE SCRIPTURES TO DIG

- Check out these other Scripture references that mention running: **2 Timothy 4:6-8**, **Galatians 5:7**, **Philippians 2:16**, **Isaiah 40:28-31**, and **Hebrews 12:1**. Check out how *The Message* translates that last verse: "Strip down, start running—and never quit! No extra spiritual fat, no parasitic sins."

- Read **Acts 2:42-47** to catch the intensity that filled Christians in the early days of the church. Those believers were convinced Jesus had risen, they were empowered by the Holy Spirit, and they were determined to soar with God and spread his Good News to the world.

18. NOT SO STRONG

You can be weak

2 Corinthians 12:10

That is why, for Christ's sake, I delight in weaknesses, in insults, in hardships, in persecutions, in difficulties. For when I am weak, then I am strong.

START You might assume from the last study that the apostle Paul was physically ripped and ready to race. Most Bible scholars, however, picture him as a man troubled by health issues and pained by beatings he'd received because of his Christian beliefs. Although Paul might not have been physically overpowering, this feisty teacher fought his entire life for his faith in Christ. He obviously got strength from someone other than himself. And he wasn't afraid to admit he often felt weak.

Feeling weak in any way—physically, emotionally, mentally, relationally, spiritually—isn't much fun. But how could it be good for your relationship with Jesus?

READ 2 Corinthians 12:7-10

> [7] Therefore, in order to keep me from becoming conceited, I was given a thorn in my flesh, a messenger of Satan, to torment me. [8] Three times I pleaded with the Lord to take it away from me. [9] But he said to me, "My grace is sufficient for you, for my power is made perfect in weakness." Therefore I will boast all the more gladly about my weaknesses, so that Christ's power may rest on me. [10] That is why, for Christ's sake, I delight in weaknesses, in insults, in hardships, in persecutions, in difficulties. For when I am weak, then I am strong.

THINK Paul just finished describing a trip "a man" took to heaven (2 Corinthians 12:1-6). It's clear Paul was talking about himself, but he didn't want to brag. So what was bothering Paul in this passage?

The Bible doesn't offer enough biographical detail to let us determine exactly what Paul was dealing with. Scholars have suggested everything from persecution to depression to malaria, epilepsy, or eye problems. Whatever it was, Paul's problem hit hard enough that he begged God to take it away. Not once, but three times.

What does God say when Paul asks him to make the problem go away? Why would God answer like that?

How is Paul going to live his life from now on? What will he do with his problems?

LIVE How can feeling strong and powerful impact your relationship with God? Does it help—or harm? Explain.

Why was Paul willing to suffer? What does that phrase "for Christ's sake" have to do with it?

Is Paul's view of weaknesses, insults, hardships, persecutions, and difficulties just plain crazy? Why—or why not?

God has a plan for your life. Life can be full of difficulties. Explain how you can press on with God's plan for your life even if you feel slammed.

WRAP Paul had been a violent persecutor of the church (Acts 9:1-3) until Jesus stopped him in his tracks (Acts 9:3-6) and gave him the task of taking the Good News about Jesus to the whole world, especially to non-Jews (Acts 9:7-18). Because Paul was sure of God's plan for his life, he kept going no matter what difficulties he faced. When Paul felt weak, he found strength in God.

» MORE THOUGHTS TO MULL

- How do you feel about God when he doesn't fix your problems?

- Do you really think God wants you to feel weak at times? Why—or why not?

- When have you been down and out—sick, hurt, needy—and learned something from it? What did you discover about God?

» MORE SCRIPTURES TO DIG

- Paul dealt with enormous hardship. But in situation after situation, he survived and pursued his goal of spreading the gospel. He summed up his mission like this: "But we have this treasure in jars of clay to show that this all-surpassing power is from God and not from us. We are hard pressed on every side, but not crushed; perplexed, but not in despair; persecuted, but not abandoned; struck down, but not destroyed. We always carry around in our body the death of Jesus, so that the life of Jesus may also be revealed in our body" (**2 Corinthians 4:7-10**).

- If you didn't look at **2 Corinthians 11:16-33** back in study 4, don't miss that list of some of the difficulties Paul endured for God.

- Paul's suffering didn't always go on and on. Read **Acts 16:16-40** to see how God sprung him from jail.

19. THE BIG QUESTION

The test of your life–glorifying God

1 Corinthians 10:31

So whether you eat or drink or whatever you do, do it all for the glory of God.

START Honestly, if you've been paying attention so far, there should be a nagging question in your brain. Suppose you've become convinced God truly cares for you and indeed has a plan for your life. So you take time to discover God's path for your life. You pursue God's best goals and keep going despite trials inside and out. Nevertheless, here's the pesky question: How do you know—for sure—that you're headed where God wants?

What's your answer to that question?

READ 1 Corinthians 10:23-24 and 10:31-11:1

> [23] "I have the right to do anything," you say—but not everything is beneficial. "I have the right to do anything"—but not everything is constructive. [24] No one should seek their own good, but the good of others. [31] So whether you eat or drink or whatever you do, do it all for the glory of God. [32] Do not cause anyone to stumble, whether Jews, Greeks or the church of God— [33] even as I try to please everyone in every way. For I am not seeking my own good but the good of many, so that they may be saved. [1] Follow my example, as I follow the example of Christ.

THINK This reading starts in the middle of an argument about eating meat offered to idols. Some Christians condemned the practice, reasoning that the meat had been used to worship false gods. Others argued that because those gods weren't real, they were free to eat what they wanted. Tucked in this debate is a principle you don't want to miss.

As Christians God wants us to live according to our consciences, and some believers feel free to do things that others don't. But why shouldn't Christians always insist on exercising their freedoms?

What does it mean to make someone "stumble"?

Now here's the big principle, located in verse 31. How can you know if you're headed God's way?

What does it mean to do everything "for the glory of God"?

LIVE How does the principle of "do it all for the glory of God" tell you whether you're on the right path or not?

Suppose you're pursuing what you think is God's path for your life, but you realize your main motivation is to make yourself happy at any cost. Are you on the right path—or not? Explain.

God wants us not only to do the right thing but also to do it for the right reasons. Doing everything for God's glory might sound like a tough demand, but it offers reassurance when you wonder if you're headed the right way. If you are seeking to honor God in whatever you do, you're almost surely headed in God's direction. And in the unlikely case you happen to be way off in your understanding of God's will, you have the right attitude to let him gently point you in a better direction.

When have you felt confused about a decision? How could this principle of "do it all for the glory of God" have helped you?

WRAP It's a simple test. Are you living for yourself—or for God? Get that settled, and you can plunge ahead with confidence that you're doing what God wants.

» MORE THOUGHTS TO MULL

- Do you think that finding and following God's will is too tough to do? Why—or why not?

- Is "doing all to the glory of God" about your actions—or your attitude? Explain.

- How committed are you to living for God's honor? What holds you back?

» MORE SCRIPTURES TO DIG

- Every Christian wanders from God's path, rejecting God's best way and chasing after something less. Sometimes we run far from the path. God always offers a way back. Some memorable words from **1 John 1:8-9** say it well: "If we claim to be without sin, we deceive ourselves and the truth is not in us. If we confess our sins, he is faithful and just and will forgive us our sins and purify us from all unrighteousness." When you mess up, admit it—and then say thanks for God's forgiveness.

- You can't always undo the wrong things you do. But God wants you to get up and go on. Right after Paul wrote that knowing Jesus is his life's highest goal, he admits this: "Not that I have already obtained all this, or have already arrived at my goal, but I press on to take hold of that for which Christ Jesus took hold of me. Brothers and sisters, I do not consider myself yet to have taken hold of it. But one thing I do: Forgetting what is behind and straining toward what is ahead, I press on toward the goal to win the prize for which God has called me heavenward in Christ Jesus" (**Philippians 3:12-14**).

20. LIVE BOLDLY

Follow without fear

Joshua 1:9

"Have I not commanded you? Be strong and courageous. Do not be afraid; do not be discouraged, for the Lord your God will be with you wherever you go."

START You can't say you're living boldly for God if your body stays snug in bed. You can't claim to be following his path if you stay put when you know where you should go and what you should do. God has dreams for you, and he invites you to live them out. He knows there are days when that can be a struggle. That's why he wants to give you courage.

What kinds of courage do you need to find and follow God's plan for your life?

READ Joshua 1:1-2, 7-9

[1] After the death of Moses the servant of the Lord, the Lord said to Joshua son of Nun, Moses' aide: [2] "Moses my servant is dead. Now then, you and all these people, get ready to cross the Jordan River into the land I am about to give to them—to the Israelites. [7] "Be strong and very courageous. Be careful to obey all the law my servant Moses gave you; do not turn from it to the right or to the left, that you may be successful wherever you go. [8] Keep this Book of the Law always on your lips; meditate on it day and night, so that you may be careful to do everything written in it. Then you will be prosperous and successful. [9] Have I not commanded you? Be strong and courageous. Do not be afraid; do not be discouraged, for the Lord your God will be with you wherever you go."

THINK That passage comes from the Old Testament, right after the death of Moses, the guy who led Israel out of slavery in Egypt. You've probably seen his story in classic movies like *The Ten Commandments* or *The Prince of Egypt*. Joshua was Moses' top assistant.

Where does God want Joshua to go? To do what?

God's command sends Joshua and God's people into the land the Lord had promised to Abraham long before (Genesis 17:8). While you might think storming this "Promised Land" has nothing to do with your world, it's a vivid picture of how God wants you to take hold of all the good things he promises you.

What is Joshua supposed to do with "the Book of the Law," God's early rules for living and worship? Why do that?

What does God promise to do if Joshua and the people enter the land God has promised them?

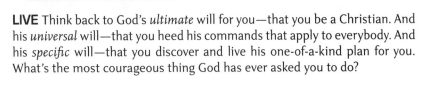

LIVE Think back to God's *ultimate* will for you—that you be a Christian. And his *universal* will—that you heed his commands that apply to everybody. And his *specific* will—that you discover and live his one-of-a-kind plan for you. What's the most courageous thing God has ever asked you to do?

What bold thing do you think God wants you to do right now? What's your next step in living out his plan for you?

What scares you most about following God's plans?

God wants you to ask him for courage to meet the challenge. Then you should plunge ahead! You have his promise to be with you. Like he told Joshua, "I will be with you. I will not leave you or forget you" (Joshua 1:5, NCV).

WRAP God knows you need courage to do his plan for your life. Jesus once compared following him to taking up a cross (Matthew 16:24). He also said the path to following him is narrow, and few are willing to walk it (Matthew 7:13-14). Making the choice to follow God in all things is the toughest challenge you can ever face. But you can face that challenge when you're sure God is with you. And he is—he's with you wherever he commands you to go.

» MORE THOUGHTS TO MULL

- Who can help you stay on track with God's plans for your life?

- When have you obeyed a difficult command—and discovered it was worth the struggle?

- Talk to God about the toughest things you will face today as you follow him—and thank him that he is with you.

» MORE SCRIPTURES TO DIG

- Study **Joshua 6** to see how the Israelites depended on God as they entered the Promised Land.

- There's a kid song you might have picked up in Sunday school. It says, "Twelve men went to spy on Canaan. Ten were bad and two were good." Joshua and his friend Caleb were the only two soldier-spies who believed God could help them conquer the land he had promised them. God sentenced the doubtful Israelites to wander in the desert for forty years—until they died—then appointed Joshua as the man to lead the Israelites onward. Read about it in **Numbers 13-14**.

In the Higher series, you'll find deep, interactive studies to help high school students engage with the Bible and develop a passionate, life-altering relationship with God. Each book has 20 studies, focusing on discipleship topics that are most relevant to high schoolers, and gets students to explore and study God's Word. In a voice that doesn't speak down to students, you'll find that these studies draw teens in and take them deeper into their faith.

Follow
Walk in the Rhythm of Jesus
978-0-310-28264-8

Think
Figure Out What You Believe and Why
978-0-310-28266-2

Soar
Fly into God's Plan for Your Future
978-0-310-28267-9

Thrive
Dare to Live Like God
978-0-310-28265-5

Kevin Johnson
Retail $8.99 each

Visit www.youthspecialties.com
or your local bookstore.

youth
specialties

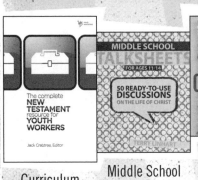

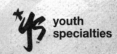